PRESCHOOL L[...]
TO LEARN ABOUT
JESUS

by

Cindy Burleson

and

Linda McRea

illustrated by Corbin Hillam

Cover by Corbin Hillam

Copyright © 1993

Shining Star Publications

ISBN No. 0-86653-767-8

Printing No. 987

Shining Star
A Division of Frank Schaffer Publications, Inc.
23740 Hawthorne Blvd.
Torrance, CA 90505-5927

Unless otherwise indicated, the New International Version of the Bible was used in preparing the activities in this book.

DEDICATION

To my husband, Richard, and son, Benjamin, I thank you for giving me the time to dedicate myself in serving the Lord in this capacity.

Linda McRea

To my husband, Tom, and my son, Thomas, for their patient and loving support during this special time of service to the Lord. Also, to my mother, Anna, for her Christian values she instilled in me as a child.

Cindy Burleson

SS380

TO THE TEACHER/PARENT

Preschool Lessons to Learn About Jesus offers a walk through the life of Jesus while providing preschoolers the opportunity to learn basic Christian values. The eight chapters include: The Birth of Jesus, The Boy Jesus, Jesus Chooses Helpers, Jesus Calms the Storm, He Is Risen, plus three others.

A Bible story introduces each chapter. Flannel board patterns, story wheels, participation stories, chalk talks, glove puppets, pop-out pictures, and stick puppets are all used to make the Bible stories come alive for your youngsters. Developmentally appropriate activities follow each story and include: finger plays, songs, crafts, games, recipes, and party suggestions.

Each activity was especially designed for preschool children. The ideas can be incorporated into any style of teaching. For example, each activity can be used individually, in small groups, or in a learning center. The material can also be tailored to your individual age group. For example, a four-year-old may need help cutting patterns that a five-year-old will enjoy cutting, while a six-year-old may want to design his own patterns. You, the teacher, will know the best ways to use the ideas found in *Preschool Lessons to Learn About Jesus.*

Remember, as you teach the children to love Jesus, let your love for the Savior be seen in you. You are a shining example. They may not always remember every word you teach, but they are always watching and learning the examples you set. You have an important challenge before you. It is vital to lay a strong Christian foundation at an early age. What could be more important than teaching a child about God? Best wishes and may God bless your teaching.

TABLE OF CONTENTS

THE BIRTH OF JESUS

A Flannel Board Story

Matthew 2:1-12; Luke 1:26-39, 2:8-20

Use figures below and on pages 7-8 for a flannel board story.

In the city of Nazareth lived a young woman named Mary. (*Place figure of Mary on flannel board.*) Mary loved God with all her heart. She was soon to marry a man named Joseph. One wonderful day God sent an angel named Gabriel to Mary. "Hello, Mary," Gabriel said. "God is pleased with you!" (*Place figure of Gabriel on board.*) Mary could hardly believe her eyes and ears. At first she was frightened. The angel said, "Do not be afraid, Mary. God loves you very much." Then he told Mary, "You are going to have a baby boy. Name Him Jesus. He will be the Son of God." She was pleased and happy that she was going to be the mother of such a special baby. Suddenly, the angel was gone. (*Remove Gabriel.*) Mary did not forget the words the angel had spoken to her. She married Joseph, and they were very happy. (*Place Joseph on board.*)

SS3801

One day Mary and Joseph had to go to the city of Bethlehem to be taxed.(*Replace Mary with Mary on donkey*.) It was getting dark when they got to Bethlehem. They wanted to stay in a nice, warm inn with a soft bed and hot food to eat.

Joseph knocked on the inn door. "We have traveled all the way from Nazareth, and my wife is very tired," he said to the innkeeper. The innkeeper said he did not have a room and he was sure there were no rooms left in the city. Joseph told him Mary was going to have a baby. "Well," said the innkeeper, "you may stay in the stable where the cows and donkeys sleep." So Joseph and Mary spent the night in the stable with the animals. (*Replace Mary on donkey with standing Mary.*) That night in the stable, Baby Jesus was born. (*Add baby in manger.*) Mary wrapped Him in some cloth and placed Him in a manger filled with hay.

On the hills outside Bethlehem it was dark and quiet. Shepherds were watching over their sleeping sheep. (*Place shepherds and sheep on board far from stable scene.*) Suddenly, they saw a bright light! An angel told the shepherds not to be afraid because he had good news that would bring happiness to everyone. He said that Jesus, God's Son, had been born in Bethlehem. Then suddenly there were many angels praising God for sending His Son, Jesus! As suddenly as they had appeared, the angels left. The shepherds hurried to see the baby sleeping in a manger-bed. (*Move shepherds next to baby.*) He was so tiny and sweet. On their way back to their sheep, they told everyone that God had sent His Son.

Some time after Jesus was born in Bethlehem, some wise men visited King Herod. They told the king that they had followed a bright star in the east to find the Baby Jesus and worship Him. (*Add star over manger scene. Remove shepherds and sheep. Place wise men far from stable scene.*) King Herod asked the wise men to go and find the baby, then come back and tell him where He was.

The wise men followed the twinkling star to Jesus. (*Move wise men next to baby.*) When they saw Him, they bowed down before Him and gave Him gifts—gold, incense, and myrhh.

An angel told the wise men in a dream not to go back and tell King Herod where Baby Jesus was. So they went home another way. (*Remove all figures.*)

Due to the length of this story, you may choose to tell it in two parts.

FLANNEL BOARD PATTERNS

Copy each pattern on pages 5-8, color with markers, and cut out. Cut the same shape from tagboard and glue it to the back of the original pattern. Cut a piece of flannel and glue it to the back of each figure.

SS3801

FLANNEL BOARD PATTERNS

SS3801

LIFE-SIZED CAMEL

Materials:

Feel O' Fleece Textural Fiber™

Sawhorse

Plywood or tagboard

Large moveable eyes

Material or felt

Fringe

Hot glue gun

Two small pillows

Staple gun

Rope

Directions:

1. Cut a camel's head from a large sheet of tagboard. (You may choose to enlarge the camel head pattern on page 14.)

2. Hot glue moveable eyes to the camel's face.

3. Cut a slot in the end of a pre-assembled sawhorse large enough to slip the camel's head in. Secure with glue if necessary.

4. Staple pillows to the top of the camel's "body" to form humps.

5. Cover pillows with material or a blanket. (You may add fringe to the material to decorate it.)

6. Wrap fleece around the camel's "legs and neck." Secure with staples or hot glue.

7. Attach a rope to the end of the sawhorse for the camel's "tail."

SS3801

SONG AND ACTION SONG

Song
Tune: "Mary Had a Little Lamb"

Mary had Baby Jesus, Baby Jesus, Baby Jesus
Mary had Baby Jesus
To take care of us.

Song
Tune: "London Bridge"

Mary and Joseph went to Bethlehem,
Went to Bethlehem, went to Bethlehem,
Mary and Joseph went to Bethlehem
To pay taxes.

(Pretend to ride a donkey.)

In a stable Jesus was born.
Jesus was born, Jesus was born,
In a stable Jesus was born
That same evening.

(Rock arms holding Baby Jesus.)

Next the angels told the shepherds,
Told the shepherds, told the shepherds,
Next the angels told the shepherds
They saw Jesus.

(Tell the good news with hands facing outward around mouth.)

Then the wise men followed the star,
Followed the star, followed the star,
Then the wise men followed the star
To see the King.

(Look up, shading eyes with hand, to follow the star.)

SS3801

MY CHRISTMAS STORYBOOK

Copy and cut out the pictures below and on page 12. Assemble them in the proper order and staple them together to form a storybook.

My Christmas Storybook

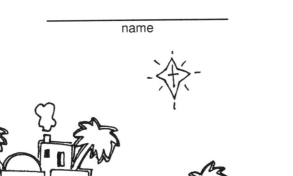

_____
name

The angel told Mary the good news.

Mary and Joseph went to Bethlehem.

There were no rooms in the inn.

MY CHRISTMAS STORYBOOK

Jesus was born in a stable.

The angels told the shepherds that Jesus was born.

The shepherds came to see Jesus.

Wise men followed a star to Jesus.

Shining Star Publications, Copyright © 1993

SS3801

PAPER PLATE CAMEL

Materials:
Tagboard
Paper plate
Black yarn
Scissors
Glue

Directions:
1. Reproduce the camel patterns on this page and page 14 on tagboard and cut them out.
2. If possible, laminate the pieces or cover them with clear adhesive plastic.
3. Cut a paper plate in half.
4. Glue the camel head on the left end of the half plate, the legs on the bottom, and the coat on the camel's "back."
5. Glue a small strand of black yarn to the right end of the plate and glue the camel's tail to it.
6. Optional: Punch a hole at the top of the camel's back and attach yarn so it can be hung as a decoration.

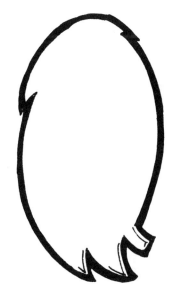

Tail

Camel coat

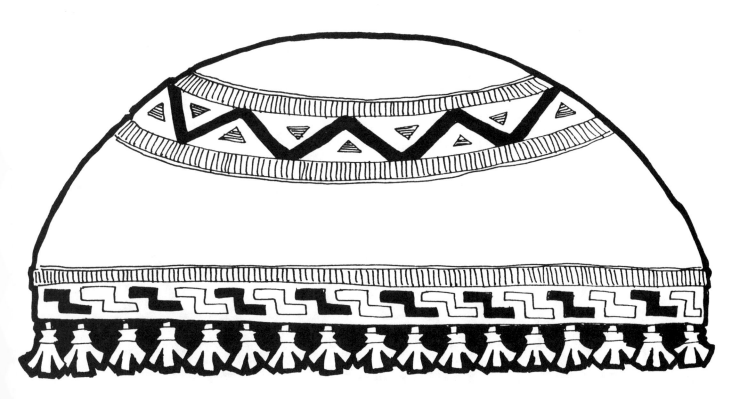

SS3801

PAPER PLATE CAMEL PATTERNS

Camel legs

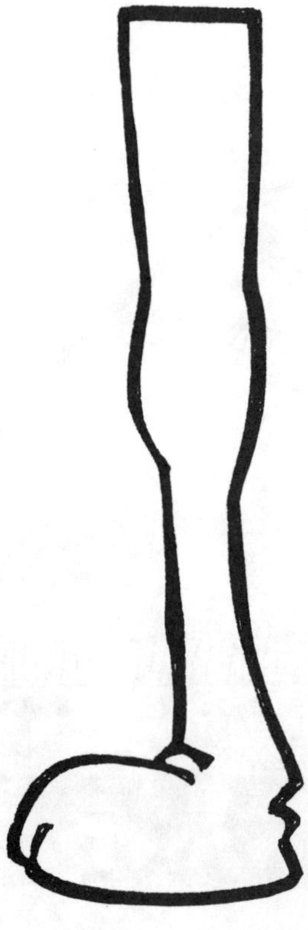

Camel head

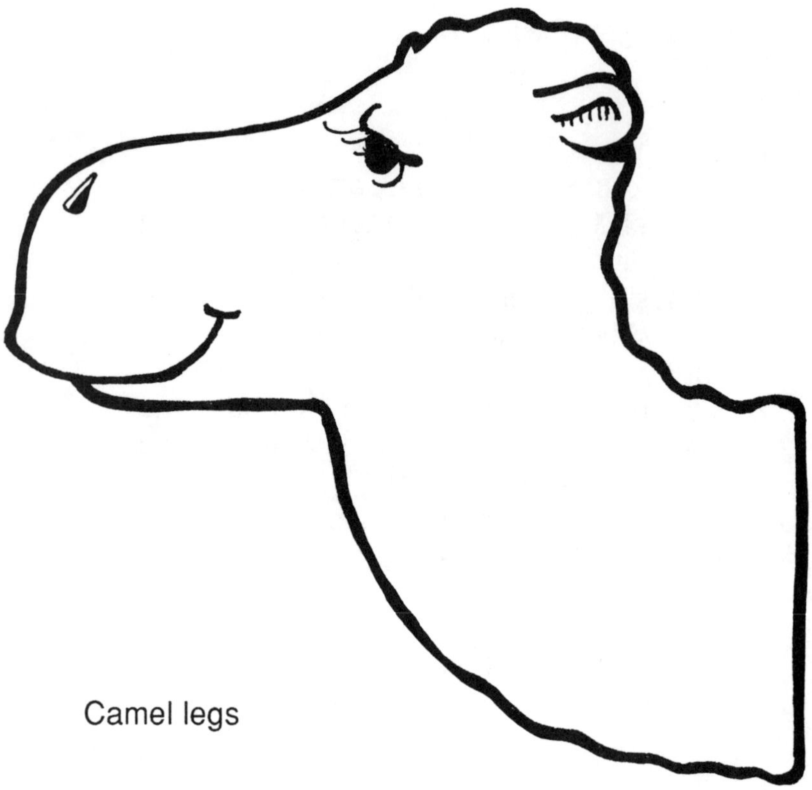

Camel legs

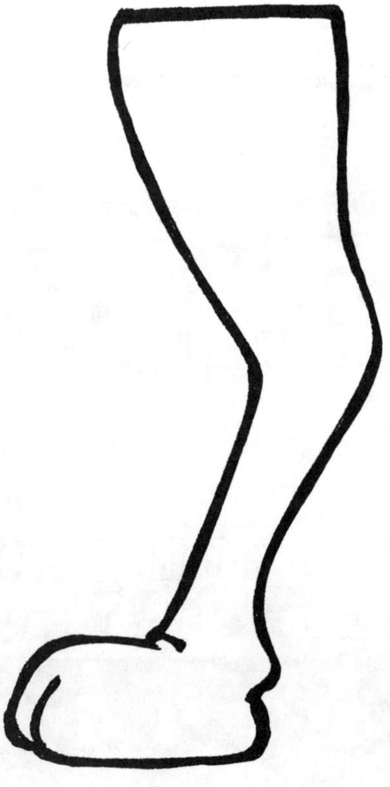

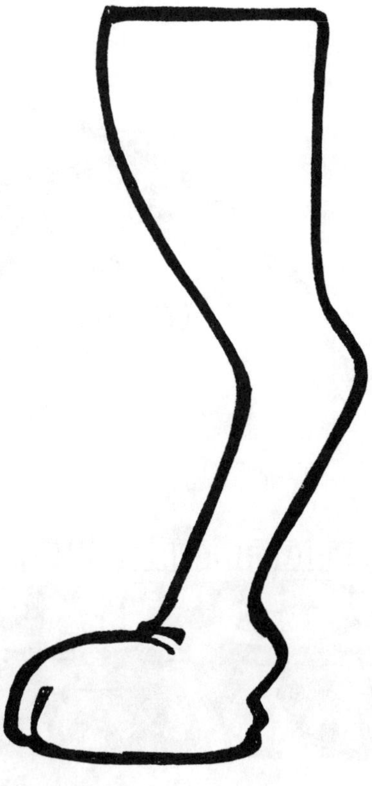

SS3801

"FOLLOW THE STAR" PARTY

Celebrate the birth of Jesus with a "follow the star" party. Serve star-shaped cookies and star-shaped cakes (recipes below). For party favors, make star ornaments ahead of time (directions on page 16) and pass them out at the party. Play camel races with stick horses (directions on page 16).

Star Cookie Recipe

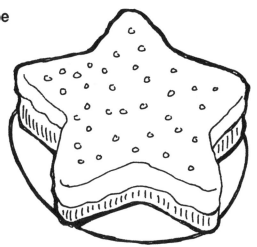

Materials:
Refrigerated sugar cookie dough
Party sprinkles

Directions:
Roll out cookie dough on a floured board and cut with a star-shaped cookie cutter. Decorate with cookie sprinkles. Bake as directed on the package.

Star-Shaped Cake

Materials:
1 package cake mix
1 can lemon frosting

Directions:
1. Prepare the cake mix according to the directions.
2. Pour batter equally into a rectangular cake pan and a round cake pan.
3. When cool, cut the rectangular cake as shown below. Place the tips around the round cake to form a star. Cover with frosting.

1.

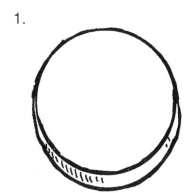

Round cake

2.

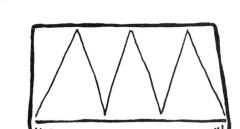

Cut rectangular cake as shown.

3.

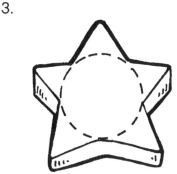

Place round cake in center.

Star Ornament

Materials:

4 cups flour   Paper clips
1 cup salt   Shellac
1¾ cups water   Brush
Star-shaped cookie cutter   Polaroid™ camera and film
Knife   Glue

Directions:

1. Make baker's clay, using the flour, salt, and water. Roll dough out ¼" thick and cut out stars.
2. With a knife, cut out the center, following the star shape.
3. Insert a paper clip in one point, to form a hook for hanging.
4. Take pictures of the children as they arrive. Cut the pictures to fit the stars. Glue to the backs of the stars.

Let the children take these party favors home to hang on their Christmas trees.

Camel Stick Horse

Enlarge this camel head and make several copies. Place on dowels. Let the children ride these camels like stick horses. Use for the lesson on the wise men visiting Jesus and for fun races.

SS3801

THE BOY JESUS

Luke 2:40-52

Use the story wheel on pages 18-19 to illustrate this story.

Every day Jesus grew to be a bigger boy. He was a good son. He obeyed Mary and probably helped Joseph in his carpenter's shop. Jesus was twelve years old when He was allowed to go with His parents to Jerusalem for the Feast of the Passover. It was a time when people went to the temple to learn about God and worship Him.

Many people went on this long trip. Most of them walked. Finally they reached Jerusalem. They prayed, studied, and worshiped God.

Mary and Joseph started back home with friends and family. They thought Jesus was in the group, but He was not. Mary looked for Jesus. Joseph looked for Jesus. Where was He? He always obeyed, and He would never run off from His mother. The next day Mary and Joseph went all the way back to Jerusalem to find Jesus. They were very worried. Where was He?

On the third day, Mary and Joseph found Jesus. He was in the temple, His Father's house. Jesus was asking the teachers questions. They were surprised that He was so smart. Mary asked Him why He had done this. She told Jesus how they had looked everywhere for Him. Jesus answered, "Didn't you know I would be in My Father's house?"

He went back home with Mary and Joseph and obeyed them, as He grew up and became wiser.

SS3801

STORY WHEEL

Materials:
  Tagboard
  Paper fastener (brad)
  Glue
  Markers
  Scissors

Directions:

1. Cut two circles, 12" in diameter, from tagboard, or use two 12" paper plates.
2. Copy and cut out the pictures from page 19, and glue them on one of the circles.
3. Cut out the temple scene below and glue it to the other circle. Cut out the temple door, so the pictures on the first circle will show through.
4. Place the temple door circle on top of the picture circle. Put a paper fastener in the center to hold the circles together. Turn the bottom "wheel" as you tell the Bible story. Children will see the story of the boy Jesus in the temple door.

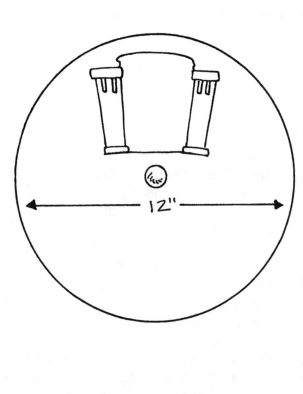

Shining Star Publications, Copyright © 1993

SS3801

1.

2.

3.

4.

SS3801

ILLUSTRATED SONG

Materials:
- Paper plate
- Craft stick
- Glue
- Scissors
- Tagboard

Directions:
1. Reproduce the faces below.
2. Glue faces to paper plates.
3. Attach craft sticks as handles to the backs of paper plates.

Tune: "Mulberry Bush"

This is the way my mother looks,
My mother looks, my mother looks,
This is the way my mother looks,
When I don't do my best (*hold up sad face*).

This is the way my mother looks,
My mother looks, my mother looks,
This is the way my mother looks,
When I do my best (*hold up happy face*).

This is the way my daddy looks . . . when I don't obey (*when I do obey*).

This is the way Jesus looks . . . when I come to church (*when I don't come to church*).

SS3801

"HAPPY HOUSE" GAME

Materials:
Tagboard
Index cards
Glue
Stapler
Scissors

Directions:
1. Reproduce the houses and glue them on tagboard.
2. Fold a piece of tagboard in half and staple both sides to form a pocket. Glue a pocket on the back of each house.
3. Reproduce each picture on page 22 and glue on an index card.
4. Have children place each picture in the appropriate house pocket. Additional cards can be made by cutting pictures from magazines and gluing them to index cards.

Happy house   Sad house

SS3801

Would these actions make the house happy or sad?

(Not sharing would make the house sad.)

(Putting away toys would make the house happy.)

(Fighting would make the house sad.)

(Going to church would make the house happy.)

 SS3801

THE BOY JESUS AT THE TEMPLE

Cut out these figures.
Have children glue them
to the picture above.

Scroll

Doves

Mary and Joseph

Teachers

 SS3801

GROW A FAMILY TREE

Materials:
Construction paper
White paper
Scissors
Glue

Directions:
1. Reproduce and cut out the tree on page 25 and the family members below for each child.
2. Let each child glue a tree on a sheet of construction paper.
3. Let each child choose figures to represent his family, and glue them on the tree.
4. Children may also add thumbprint apples to decorate the tree.
5. Reproduce and cut out the figures of Jesus and His family on page 25 for each child. As children glue the figures to the trunks of their trees, point out that each family learns and grows together.

Daddy   Mommy

Brother   Sister   Baby

FAMILY TREE PATTERNS

Mary

Joseph

Jesus

SS3801

FAMILY DAY CELEBRATION

Invite each child's family to celebrate family day at the end of this study unit.

FAMILY RECIPE

Ask parents to bring their favorite family recipe.

FAMILY PHOTO

Ask parents to bring a baby photo of their child. Have your class guess which picture goes with each child.

FAMILY APPRECIATION CARD

Let each child prepare a special card for her family to give to her parents at the party.

FAMILY INVITATION

You are invited to Family Day.

Place:

Time:

Date:

Please come and help us praise God for families.

SS3801

THE PRODIGAL SON

Luke 15:11-31

This participation story may be told using stick figures for home, father, younger son, and pigs. Directions and patterns may be found on pages 28-29.

HOME FATHER YOUNGER SON PIGS

One day, Jesus told a story about a who had two sons. The took

care of his sons, and saved some money for them. Then the decided to

leave his and travel to exciting places. This made the sad, but

he gave his half of the money he had saved. The left

 and spent most of his money with his bad friends doing wrong things.

When he ran out of money, the only job he could get was feeding   . The

 went , but he was afraid his would be mad

at him. Then he saw that his was happy to see him and thankful that his

 was back . The told his that

he was sorry for leaving him and spending all of the money. The forgave

his

   SS3801

STORY ON A STICK PATTERNS

The story on a stick is an excellent method to use to illustrate the adventure of the prodigal son while encouraging participation. Read the story aloud as you hold up the figures of home, father, younger son, and pig. To reinforce the story, let children hold up the figures as you retell it.

Materials:
Tagboard
Craft sticks
Scissors
Glue

Directions:
1. Reproduce each figure on tagboard.
2. Color each figure and cut it out.
3. If possible, laminate each figure.
4. Glue each figure on a craft stick.

Pig

Home

SS3801

Prodigal Son

Father

29

SS3801

CIRCLE STORY CHALK TALK

Draw the sketch shown below as you tell the story, connecting the pictures with a continuous line until the son ends up back where he began, at the beginning of the circle.

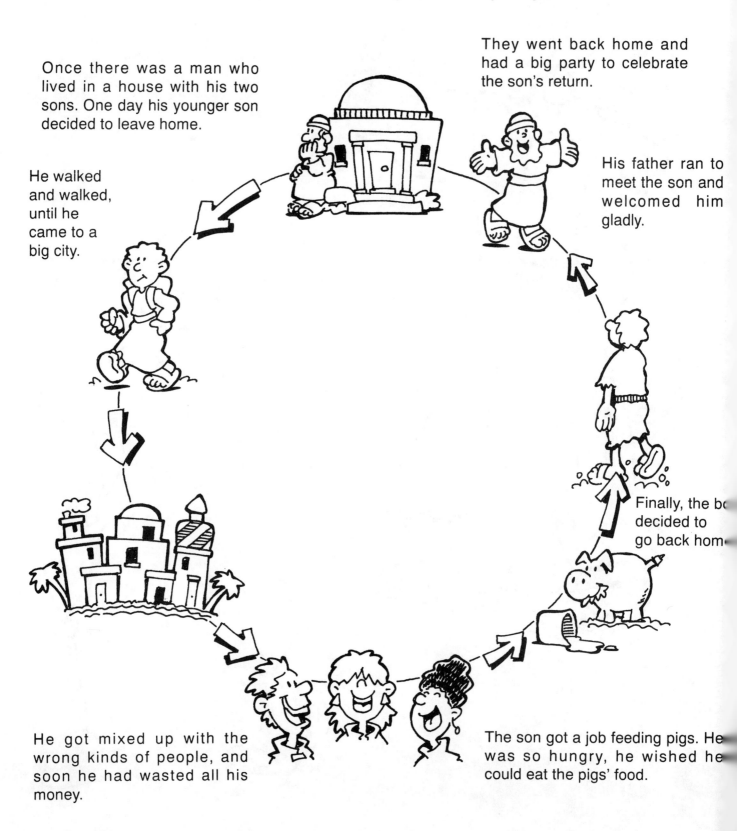

Once there was a man who lived in a house with his two sons. One day his younger son decided to leave home.

They went back home and had a big party to celebrate the son's return.

He walked and walked, until he came to a big city.

His father ran to meet the son and welcomed him gladly.

Finally, the boy decided to go back home.

He got mixed up with the wrong kinds of people, and soon he had wasted all his money.

The son got a job feeding pigs. He was so hungry, he wished he could eat the pigs' food.

SS3801

SONG, RHYME, AND FINGERPLAY

Song
Tune: "This Old Man"

This young son he left home
He spent everything he owned
With wild friends and parties,
Then he had no food,
So this son came running home.

Rhyme

This little pig went to the field.
This little pig stayed in the pen.
This little pig had supper,
But this young son had none.
The son cried "I have sinned,"
All the way home.

Fingerplay
Tune: "Ten Little Indians"

One little, two little, three little pigs, (*count with fingers*)
Four little, five little, six little pigs, (*count with fingers*)
Seven little, eight little, nine little pigs, (*count with fingers*)
Ten little hungry pigs. (*count with fingers*)

Ten little, nine little, eight little pigs, (*count with fingers*)
Seven little, six little, five little pigs, (*count with fingers*)
Four little, three little, two little pigs, (*count with fingers*)
One pig left to feed. (*count with fingers*)

There's no food for the Prodigal Son, (*shake head, no*)
There's no food for the Prodigal Son, (*shake head, no*)
There's no food for the Prodigal Son, (*shake head, no*)
So he must go home. (*use first finger and index finger like walking*)

His father was happy to see him, (*point to smiling face*)
His father was happy to see him, (*point to smiling face*)
His father was happy to see him, (*point to smiling face*)
He forgave his son. (*hug yourself*)

SS3801

PIGPEN GAMES

Materials:
    Berry basket or small containers for pigpens
    Tagboard or construction paper
    Scissors
    Glue

Pig Pattern Directions:
1. On pink tagboard, reproduce the pig pattern found below. Make fifty-five pigs.
2. Cut out the pigs.

Pig Counting Game
1. Write the numerals 1-10 on construction paper circles.
2. Attach one circle to the side of every berry basket pigpen.
3. Have children drop the correct number of pigs in each pen.

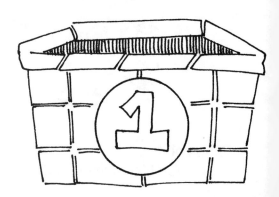

Question and Answer Game
Use the berry basket pigpens to keep score of correctly answered questions. Each child or team gets a berry basket pigpen. As you ask questions relating to the Prodigal Son story, children take turns answering. Each time a student gives a correct answer, he gets to drop a pig in his pen.

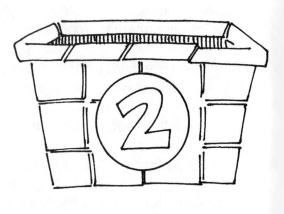

SS3801

"WELCOME HOME, SON" GAME

Copy the pig marker and give one to each child to color a different color. Have children take turns flipping a coin and moving the pig ahead two spaces for heads and one space for tails. If a child lands on a space with an arrow, he must move backward on his next turn. The picture located beside each arrow illustrates why the son didn't make progress in his life. Discuss the obstacles the son faced.

Pig Marker

SS3801

PIG MATCHING ACTIVITY

Cross out the picture in each row that doesn't match. Color the matching pictures the same color.

SS3801

PRODIGAL SON FESTIVAL

"Celebrate and be glad . . . he was lost and is found."   Luke 15:32

Party Balloons

Materials:
Pink construction paper
Black marker
Pink balloon
Scissors
String
Glue

Directions:
1. Inflate a pink balloon. Attach string to the bottom of the balloon.
2. Cut two ears from pink construction paper and glue them to the top of the balloon.
3. Draw eyes and nose with a black marker.

Party Masks

Materials:
Pink construction paper
Black marker
Hole punch
Paper cup
Scissors
Yarn
Glue

Directions:
1. Cut and glue pink construction paper circles to fit the end of the paper cup.
2. Draw black nostrils in the middle of the nose.
3. Punch a hole in each side of the paper cup as shown.
4. Insert yarn through the holes to tie at the back of child's head.

Shining Star Publications, Copyright © 1993
SS3801

Party Treats

Pig Cupcakes

Bake cupcakes as directed on cake mix box. When cool, spread with cherry or strawberry icing. Cut two ears from pink construction paper and insert on top of the cupcake. Decorate with miniature marshmallow eyes, chocolate kisses, jelly bean noses, etc.

Pigs 'n' Mud
Instant chocolate pudding
Tube of sugar cookie dough
Pig-shaped cookie cutter

Make chocolate pudding according to directions on the box, or let children shake instant pudding mix and milk in sealed glass jars until thick.

On a floured board, roll out the cookie dough. Cut with the pig-shaped cookie cutter and bake as directed on the package.

Put pudding in small bowls and stand a pig in each.

Pigs 'n' Blankets
Can of biscuits
Party sausages

Wrap each precooked sausage in a biscuit and bake according to the directions on the biscuit can.

SS3801

JESUS CHOOSES HELPERS

Matthew 4:18-22; Luke 6:12-16

Use the "Jesus and His Helpers" paper plate visual on page 38 to illustrate this story.

Jesus (*hold up the paper plate face of Jesus*) had much work to do. He needed help in taking God's Word to the world. Jesus prayed and asked God to help Him choose the best men to help Him with His work.

Jesus liked to walk beside the Sea of Galilee. One day as He was walking, He saw two fishermen (*pull out the first two helper faces*). They were brothers, and were known to be good men. They were Peter and his brother, Andrew. Jesus called to them, "Come and follow Me. I will make you fishers of men." Peter and Andrew decided to be helpers. They left their boat and followed Jesus.

Peter, Andrew, and Jesus walked on. They came to two more fishermen (*pull the next two faces out*). They were sitting in a boat, fixing their nets. These two men were brothers too. Their names were James and John. Jesus called to them as He had to Peter and Andrew. They, too, left their nets and followed Jesus.

Later, Jesus passed a tax office where He met a man named Matthew (*pull another face out*), who worked there. "Follow Me," Jesus said. Matthew got up and followed Jesus.

Altogether, Jesus asked twelve men to be His helpers and serve the Lord. Besides Peter, Andrew, James, John, and Matthew, there were Bartholomew, Thomas, another man named James, Simon, Thaddaeus, and Judas. (*As you say each helper's name, pull out one face until all are showing.*)

SS3801

PAPER PLATE VISUAL

Materials:
Paper plate
Ribbon
Tape
Glue
Scissors
Stapler

Directions:
1. Cut the paper plate in half. Staple the two halves together, leaving the top open.
2. Reproduce the face of Jesus on page 39, and glue it to the front of the paper plate.
3. Cut a piece of ribbon 24" long.
4. Reproduce the faces of the twelve helpers below. Glue them on the ribbon 1" apart.
5. Tape the ribbon inside the plate ½" from the top. Place the ribbon inside the plate pocket.
6. Pull the ribbon out and show the faces one by one as you tell the story.

SS3801

Jesus

SS3801

CHALK TALK

Draw the lines shown below as you tell the story, and have a completed picture of a fish when you're done.

1. One day, Jesus was walking by the Sea of Galilee. He saw a boat there.

2. Jesus stood on the shore and called out to the men in the boat. Peter and Andrew were fishing in the boat.

3. Jesus called to them, "Come and follow Me." The men did as Jesus asked. They followed Him here. They followed Him there.

4. As Jesus was walking along, He saw James and John and they also followed Him. Altogether, Jesus asked twelve men to be His helpers. Peter, Andrew, James, and John fished for fish, but Jesus told His twelve helpers to be fishers of men.

SS3801

HELPERS' SONGS

Tune: "Are You Sleeping"

How many helpers, how many helpers
Did He choose, did He choose
Jesus chose twelve helpers, Jesus chose twelve helpers
Yes, He did, yes, He did.

JESUS, LORD, HE CHOSE TWELVE
Tune: "This Old Man"
by Judith Capuano-Schera

Verse 1
Jesus, Lord, He chose one, (*Hold up one finger.*)
Peter, there's work to be done. (*Shake index finger.*)
Refrain
If you wish to follow Me (*Point to self with both thumbs.*)
Give up all you own. (*Raise hands overhead, palms up.*)
Heaven then shall be your home. (*Keeping hands overhead, look up.*)
Verse 2
Jesus, Lord, He chose two, (*Hold up two fingers.*)
Andrew, let's make old hearts new. (*Cross hands over heart.*)
Refrain
Verse 3
Jesus, Lord, He chose three. (*Hold up three fingers.*)
Jesus, come help make all men see. (*Place right index finger under eye.*)
Refrain
Verse 4
Jesus, Lord, He chose four. (*Hold up four fingers.*)
John, bring hope to spirits poor. (*Extend both hands, palms up.*)
Refrain
Verse 5
Jesus, Lord, He chose five. (*Hold up five fingers.*)
Matthew, keep My words alive. ("*Write*" *with right palm.*)
Refrain
Verse 6
Jesus, Lord, He chose six, (*Hold up six fingers.*)
Philip, wrong ways need be fixed. (*Fold arms in front; nod.*)
Refrain

Verse 7
Jesus, Lord, He chose seven, (*Hold up seven fingers.*)
Seek, Bartholomew, your brethren. (*Raise right hand over brows.*)
Refrain
Verse 8
Jesus, Lord, He chose eight. (*Hold up eight fingers.*)
Thomas, be My sign of faith. (*Fold hands as to pray.*)
Refrain
Verse 9
Jesus, Lord, He chose nine, (*Hold up nine fingers.*)
Jesus, embrace this soul of mine. (*Hug self.*)
Refrain
Verse 10
Jesus, Lord, He chose ten, (*Hold up ten fingers.*)
Simon, help them live again. (*Cup hands together, raise up.*)
Refrain
Verse 11
Jesus, Lord, He chose eleven, (*Hold up ten, then one finger.*)
Thaddeus, lead them to heaven. (*Point upward with right hand.*)
Refrain
Verse 12
Jesus, Lord, He chose twelve. (*Hold up ten, then two fingers.*)
Judas, you thought of yourself. (*Point out with right hand.*)
Didn't wish to follow Me (*Shade head "no."*)
Chose to stand alone. . . (*Take step back, look away.*)
Heaven cannot be your home! (*Hang head down, shake head "no."*)

Shining Star Publications, Copyright © 1993
SS3801

"WHATEVER I'LL BE" FLIP CHART

The disciples were helpers of Jesus. Enlarge these pictures and the ones on page 43 and put together a flip chart to illustrate the importance of being Christian helpers.

I could be a preacher.

I could be a mommy and housewife.

I could be a secretary.

I could be a fireman.

SS3801

I could be a teacher.

I could be an astronaunt.

I could be a handyman.

I could be a hairdresser, but whatever I am, I will be Jesus' helper.

Shining Star Publications, Copyright © 1993

SS3801

"FISHERS OF MEN" GAME

Materials:
- Large paper clip
- Magnet
- Dowel
- String
- Tagboard

Directions:
1. Reproduce occupation hats.
2. Cut out and laminate or cover with clear adhesive.
3. Attach a clip to the top of each hat.
4. Tie a string on one end of a dowel.
5. Tie a magnet on the end of the string.
6. Let children fish for occupations.

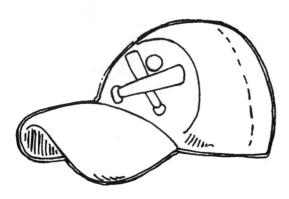

Baseball player

Construction worker

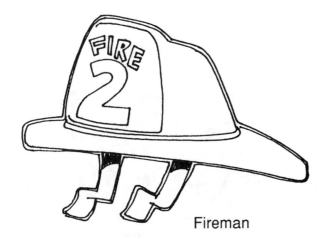

Fireman

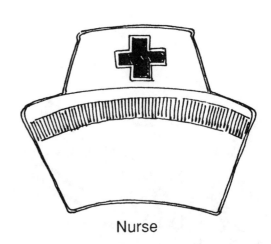

Nurse

Football player

Police officer

SS3801

"CHOOSING DISCIPLES" MATCHING GAME

Materials:
Tagboard
Index cards
Scissors
Glue

Directions:
1. Make two copies of each picture below.
2. Cut out the pictures and glue them on index cards.
3. Place the cards facedown in three rows.
4. Children take turns flipping two cards at a time until a match is found. When a child makes a match, he holds the two cards. Encourage children to tell how each picture relates to the Bible story.

"FISHERS OF MEN"
THUMBPRINTS AND GAMES

Have the children dip their fingers in finger paint, then put twelve thumbprints on a sheet of paper. When dry, use a black marker to draw faces to represent the twelve disciples.

Finger Paint Recipe
  2 cups flour
  2 tsp. salt
  3 cups cold water
  2 cups hot water
  Food color

Gradually add cold water to flour and salt. Beat until smooth. Add hot water and cook until glossy. Stir constantly. Add food color as desired. Refrigerate until ready to use.

Jesus said, "Come follow me, and I will make you fishers of men."   Matthew 4:19

Follow the Leader

Have the children play the game, follow the leader. Encourage children to take turns being the leader. The leader should say, "Follow me and I will make you fishers of men," each time he leads off the group.

John, John, James

Have the children play the game "Duck, Duck, Goose." But instead of saying "duck, duck, goose" as "It" circles the outside of the circle tapping others on the head, he should say, "John, John, James," etc. When he says James, that person stands and chases "It" around the outside of the circle. Any names of disciples may be substituted in this game.

                                       SS3801

MAKE 'N' TAKE DISCIPLE

On heavy paper, reproduce this disciple mask for each child. The child may draw a face on the mask. Glue pieces of yarn on the beard and hair. With a hole punch, make a hole on either side of the mask. Attach yarn or string so the mask may be worn by the child.

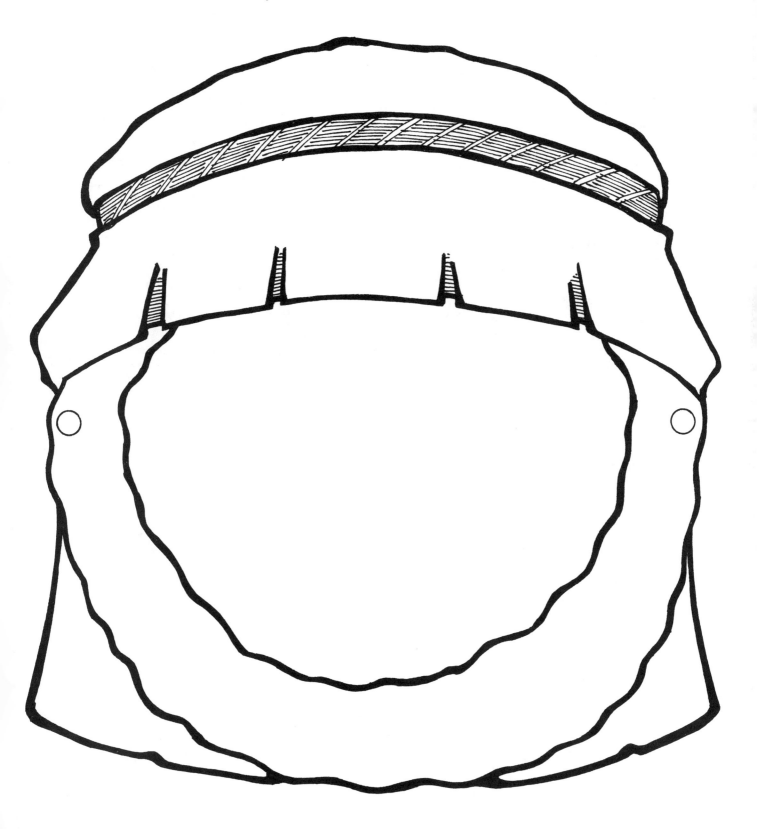

Shining Star Publications, Copyright © 1993

SS3801

FISHERS OF MEN PARTY

This party can be used to help the children become better acquainted with the people Jesus chose for His special helpers, and to teach them that He wants them to be His helpers too.

Fish Balloon

Materials:
    Tagboard
    Black marker
    Balloon
    Scissors
    Tape

Directions:
1. Inflate the balloon.
2. Using the pattern, cut two fins from tagboard and tape to the top and bottom of the fish.
3. Cut a tail from tagboard and tape it to the back of the fish.
4. Use a black marker to draw the eyes.

Fish Net Treats

Materials:
    Licorice whips
    Fish-shaped crackers

Directions:
1. Weave licorice whips to form a net.
2. Place fish-shaped crackers on the net.
3. Gather together the edges and tie with another licorice whip.

Dress Up

Encourage the chidren to bring clothes to demonstrate what they would like to be when they grow up. The children may also dress up as the disciples with masks from page 47, and robes.

JESUS CALMS THE STORM

Mark 4:35-41; Matthew 8:23-27; Luke 8:22-25

This Bible story may be illustrated with black light or flannel board silhouettes. Patterns are found on pages 50-51. The picture below may be colored with fluorescent markers. Children will enjoy looking at it under the black light. The story may also be told as a participation story. See the directions on page 52.

Jesus had been busy talking to people about God all day. (*Show figure of Jesus.*) When He finished teaching, He told His disciples that He wanted to go to the other side of the lake. Jesus and His helpers got into the boat. (*Show Jesus and helpers in boat.*) Jesus was so tired, He lay down in the boat and went to sleep. (*Show Jesus lying down.*)

After Jesus had fallen asleep, a terrible storm came up on the lake. (*Show thunder, clouds, and high waves.*) The wind began to blow. Waves crashed into the boat. Thunder began to rumble. Then the rain came down and began to fill the boat with water. Everyone was afraid! The disciples thought they were going to drown.

They woke Jesus. He told them they should not be afraid because He would take care of them. He told the storm to be still. (*Show Jesus and His helpers in boat.*) The wind stopped blowing and the waves stopped crashing. Jesus could not only make sick people well, He could also make the wind and sea obey Him!

Jesus, God's Son, does not want you to be afraid either. He will be your helper and keep you safe. You can pray any time, especially when you are afraid. Jesus is with you.

SS3801

SILHOUETTE PATTERNS

Reproduce the figures on this page and page 51 on fluorescent paper or poster board, or color them with fluorescent markers. Children will be captivated with pictures that glow in the dark. If you are using the figures with a flannel board, glue flannel to the back of each one.

Jesus

Jesus and His Helpers in Boat

SS3801

Jesus lying down in boat

Thunder and clouds

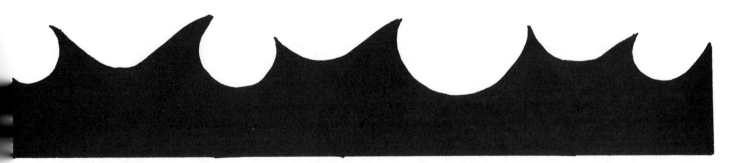

Waves

  SS3801

PARTICIPATION STORY

Jesus Calms the Storm

This is a fun, exciting way to review the story of Jesus calming the storm. Encourage children to pantomime the actions and make the sounds to help the Bible story on page 49 come to life. You may prefer to tape the sound effects and play them as you tell the story.

	Actions or Sounds
Boat	*Children hold their left arms horizontal for the boat and right arms vertical for the sail, then sway back and forth.*
Jesus sleeping in boat	*Children say "Shh" as they put index fingers to lips.*
Storm	*Children cup hands around their mouths and blow; or bang on pots and pans.*
Waves	*Children hold their arms above their heads and sway back and forth.*
Thunder	*Children clap their hands.*
Rain	*Children snap their fingers or say "pitter-patter."*
Everyone was afraid!	*Children shake all over as if in fear.*
He told the wind to be still.	*Children stand up and point.*
The wind stopped blowing and the waves stopped crashing.	*Children stand absolutely quiet.*
You can pray any time, especially when you're afraid.	*Children fold hands and bow heads.*

SS3801

IT'S TIME TO PRAY

Jesus stopped the storm when His disciples were afraid. Jesus is our friend and takes care of us. We can pray when we are afraid. These pictures about prayer (pages 53-55) may be cut out and turned into a flip chart or glued to craft sticks and shared with your students.

It's time to pray.

Let's zip up our mouths,

(Note: Glue a real zipper to the mouth.)

keep our feet still,

(Note: Glue string to the laces.)

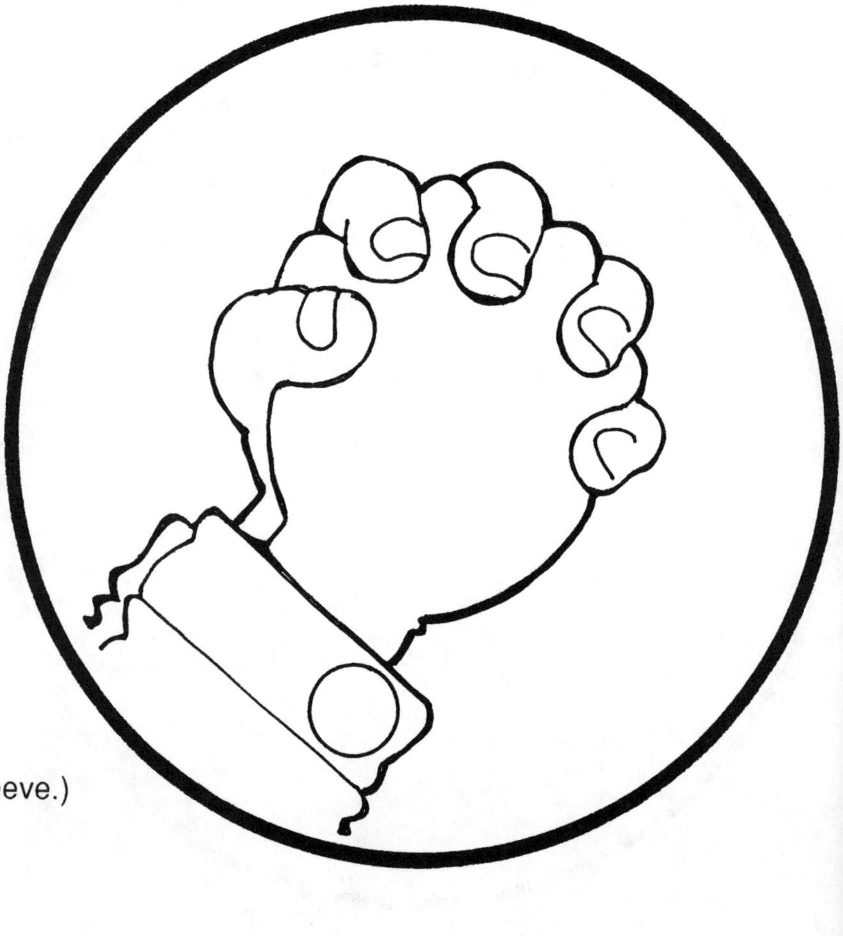

fold our hands,

(Note: Glue a button to the sleeve.)

SS3801

bow our heads,

and say, "Thank You, God, for Jesus and for Your loving care. Please be with me when I am afraid."

55

SS3801

CHARADES

We should thank God for all types of weather. God is good to us and sends us rain, wind, snow, and sunshine. The rain waters plants and flowers and the sun makes them grow. Ask children to act out the types of weather given below. Discuss the weather during the Bible story, as well as the current weather.

Windy

Rainy

Sunny

Snowy

WIND CHIME

This wind chime may be hung outside each child's home as a reminder of how Jesus told the wind to be still. Explain that Jesus can control nature because He is the Son of God.

Materials:
Seashells
Hole punch
Tagboard 8½" x 11"
Yarn
Scissors
Stapler
Glue

Directions:
1. Reproduce this sailboat for each child and cut it out. Let the child color it.
2. Roll tagboard to form a cylinder, and staple together. Glue the sailboat on the front of the cylinder.
3. Punch seven holes around the bottom of the cylinder.
4. Insert various lengths of yarn in the holes and tie them.
5. Attach a seashell to the bottom of each piece of yarn.
6. Punch a hole on the left and right side of the top of the cylinder. Insert a piece of yarn in the hole and tie to form a hanger.

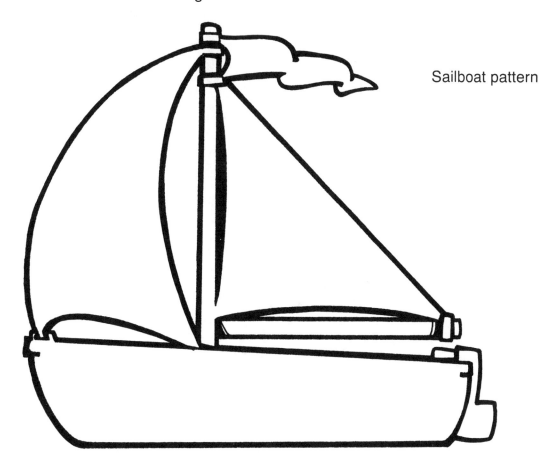

Sailboat pattern

SS3801

MAKE A BOAT

Materials:
Bar of floating soap, jar lid, or walnut shell
Paper
Toothpicks
Clay (if using a jar lid or walnut shell)
Scissors
Crayons

Directions:
1. Cut a triangle sail from paper and let the children decorate it.
2. Poke a toothpick through the sail, in one side and out the other. Leave one end of the toothpick sticking below the sail. Poke it into the bar of soap.
3. If you're using a shell or lid, poke the toothpick into a lump of clay and put the clay inside the shell or lid.

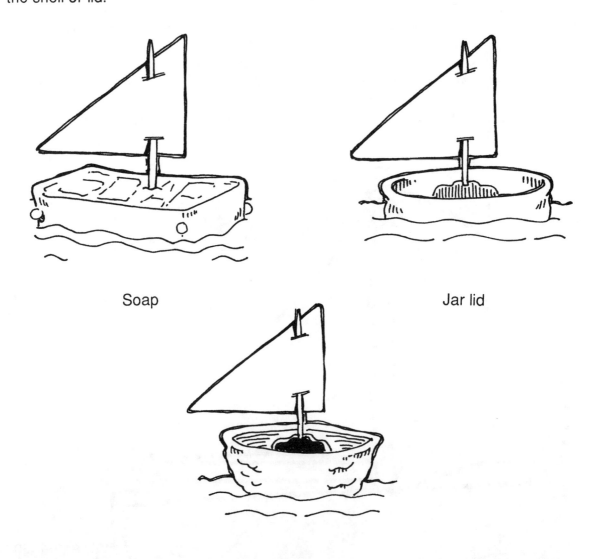

Soap   Jar lid

Walnut

SS3801

"JESUS CALMS THE STORM" CELEBRATION

Celebrate the Bible story with special treats, activities, and hats!

Sailboat Cake

Materials:
Cake pan
Cake mix
Vanilla frosting
Chocolate frosting
Shredded coconut
Blue food coloring
Licorice

Directions:
Bake a 9" by 13" sheet cake. When cool, cut as shown. Place the pieces together to form a boat shape. Frost the boat with chocolate frosting, and the sail with vanilla icing. Spread a thin layer of frosting around the sides of the boat. Add a few drops of blue food coloring to shredded coconut and sprinkle it on the frosting on the sides of the boat. Use a stick of licorice for the mast.

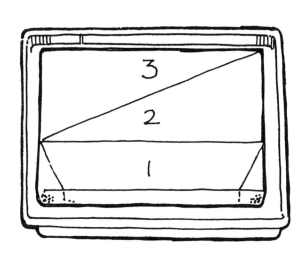 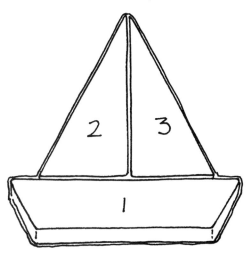

Make a Storm

Materials:
Toy boat
Water
Tub or dishpan
Alka-Seltzer™ or vinegar and baking soda

Directions:
1. Make a storm by putting an Alka-Seltzer™ in water, or ³⁄₄ cup of vinegar and 4 tsp. of baking soda in ¹⁄₄ cup of water.
2. Place a toy boat in the water. The boat will toss about in the water, simulating a storm.

Shining Star Publications, Copyright © 1993 SS3801

Sailor Hats

Materials:
    White construction paper (11" x 17")
    Stapler

Directions:
1. Fold the paper in half with the open end at the bottom.
2. Fold down the right and left corners leaving a 1" space between corners.
3. Fold up the front and back 1½" to meet the corners.

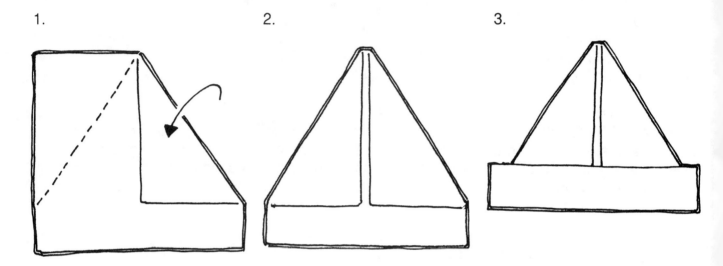

1.   2.   3.

Bottled Storm

Materials:
    Baby food jar
    Blue food coloring
    Cooking oil
    Vinegar
    Gold glitter
    Hot glue gun and glue
    Small toy boat or cork

Directions:
1. Fill the baby food jar with water.
2. Drop two drops of blue food coloring, 7 teaspoons of vinegar, and ¼ cup of cooking oil into the baby food jar. Then sprinkle gold glitter into the jar. Fill the rest of the jar with water.
3. Put the boat or cork into the water. Hot glue the lid on tightly. Rock the jar back and forth and watch the waves toss the boat around.

THE WIDOW'S OFFERING

Mark 12:38-44; Luke 21:1-4

This story may be illustrated with the glove puppet on page 62.

The temple-church was a big beautiful building where people went to worship God. One day Jesus and His helpers were at the temple. They saw people walking by with their offerings, money they wanted to give to God. Inside the temple were some money boxes. (*Show glove puppet. Hold up thumb with money box on it.*) These were open at the top so people could put their money inside.

Some rich people came up to the offering box and put lots of money in it. (*Hold up finger showing rich man.*) They wanted everyone to see them give their money to God. Their offerings did not make Jesus happy. He knew they kept most of their money for themselves.

Then a woman came up to give her money to God. (Hold up finger showing poor widow.) She was a poor widow. She did not have beautiful clothes like the rich people. She had only two coins. (*Hold up finger showing coins.*) It was all the money she had! Jesus (*Hold up finger showing Jesus*) called His helpers over to see that the poor widow had given God the very best gift. The rich people had given only part of what they had, but the poor widow showed God how thankful she was by giving Him all she had.

When we give our money in church, we show that we are thankful for all God has given us. We can also give other things, such as a smile for a visitor, a hug for a lonely person, or a colored picture to cheer up someone who is sick. God will be thankful for these gifts too.

GLOVE PUPPET

Materials:
  Glove
  Velcro™
  Hot glue gun and glue
  White paper
  Crayons
  Scissors

Directions:
1. Using a hot glue gun, attach Velcro™ to the fingertips of a glove.
2. Reproduce, color, and cut out the five pictures on this page.
3. Hot glue the Velcro™ to the pictures to attach them to the Velcro™ on the fingertips of the glove. Attach the pictures, then tell the story, raising the fingers to reveal the pictures.

Shining Star Publications, Copyright © 1993

SS380

FOLD A COIN

Fold and cut a sheet of paper as shown below. Explain to the children that the more we give to God, the more we get in return. When you "give . . . it will be given to you" (Luke 6:38). Illustrate by showing the paper coin and explaining that we give a coin to God and get many more coins or blessings in return.

Materials:
   Sheet of 8½" x 11" paper
   Scissors

Directions:
1. Fold a sheet of 8 ½" x 11" paper horizontally three times. When you are finished folding, you will have one strip approximately 1" wide.
2. Cut a coin shape in the top portion of the strip as shown. Do not cut the left and right sides of the coin, but leave them attached to the strip. Discard the rest of the paper.
3. Show the coin without unfolding it. Explain that when we give a small gift to God, He often gives us much more in return! (Unfold the strip to show many coins.)

1.

2.

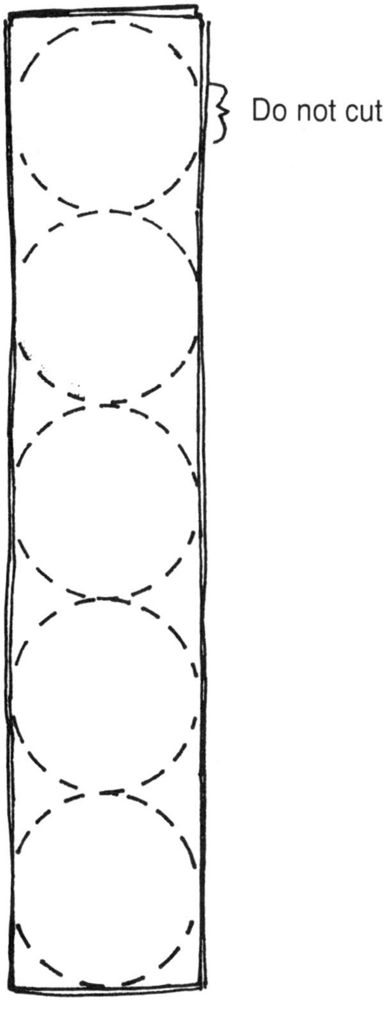

3.

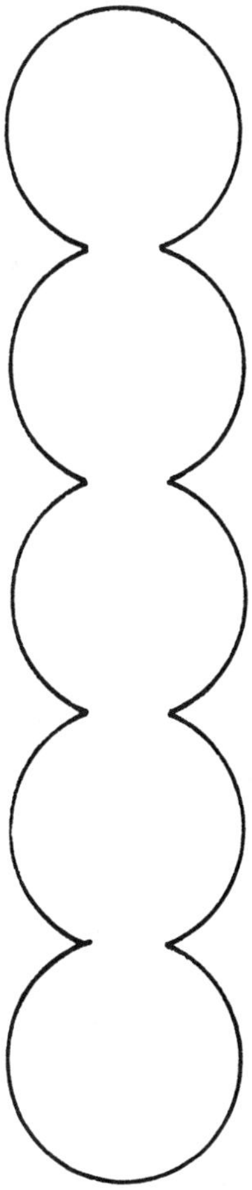

Do not cut

SS3801

"GIVING" SONGS

Tune: The Bus Song

Oh, the coins in the box went
Click, click, click
Click, click, click
Click, click, click
Oh, the coins in the box went
Click, click, click
As the widow gave.

Tune: We Get Together

The more we give to God, to God, to God
The more we give to God
The happier we'll be.

The more we give to others, to others, to others
The more we give to others
The happier we'll be.

"Giving a Song" Jar

A good way for children to give to God is through music. Emphasize that God loves for us to talk to Him by singing praises. Fill a quart jar with paper coins. Glue pictures on the backs of the coins to represent songs to sing to God. Let each child take a coin and choose a song to go along with the picture on the back. The class may give to God by singing that song.

SS3801

"GIVING" HANDS

Materials:
White paper
Construction paper
Silver paper
Glue
Markers

Directions:
1. Reproduce, color, and cut out the pairs of hands on this page and page 66.
2. Glue them to construction paper.

The poor widow's hands gave all her money.

The rich man's hands kept most of his money.

My hands can give some help to my daddy.

My hands can give some help to my mommy.

SS3801

My hands can give flowers to a sick person.

My hands can give a hug.

My hands can give a pretty picture.

My hands can give a handshake to a neighbor.

SS380

SHOPPING GAME

Use this game to teach children that each time they get money, they should set aside a portion for God. Emphasize that "God loves a cheerful giver" (2 Corinthians 9:7). This shopping game will allow your children to put that concept into practice. The church pattern and game directions are given below. The store patterns are on pages 68-69.

Materials:
Poster board
Play money
Tables
Scissors
Tape
Glue

Directions:
1. Reproduce and cut out the church and store patterns.
2. Glue them to pieces of poster board.
3. Tape each piece of poster board to the front of a table to indicate a store. As an added feature, place appropriate items or pictures of items on each store table for children to buy.
4. Give each child some play money for shopping.
5. The goal of the game is to remind children to give to God before they spend the rest of their money. Talk about how much each child should give to God and why God's money should be set aside first.

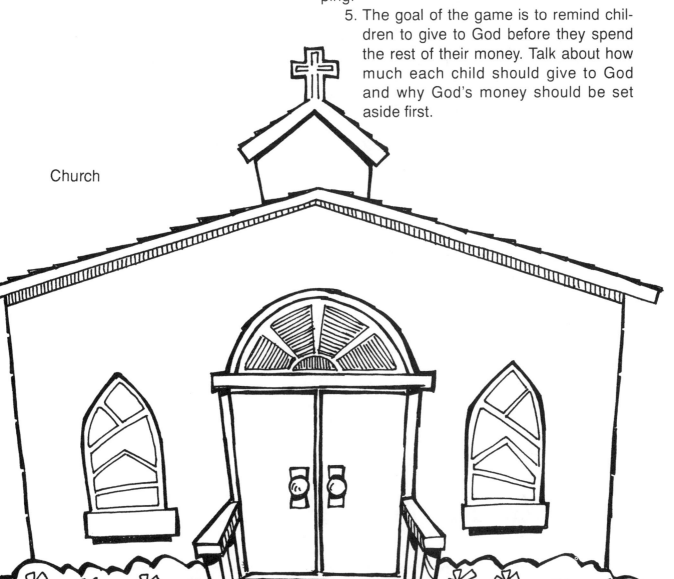

Church

STORE PATTERNS

Toy store

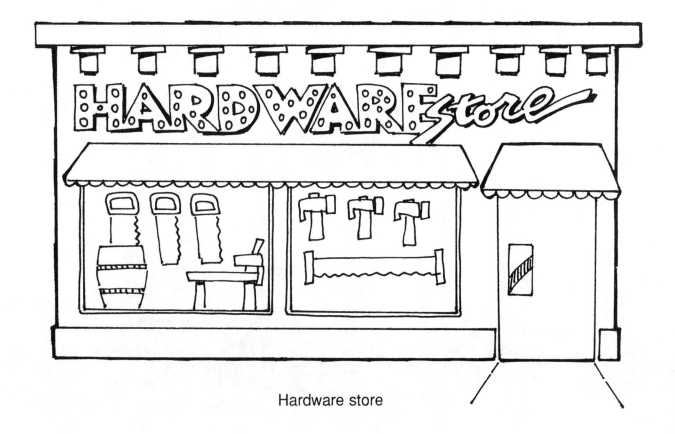

Hardware store

68

STORE PATTERNS

Clothing store

Grocery store

SS3801

"GIVING YOURSELF" CRAFT

"It is more blessed to give than to receive" (Acts 20:35). The most important aspect of giving is to give ourselves to God. This can be accomplished by singing songs of praise, helping others, giving money, and other ways. Use this craft to illustrate this concept to your children.

Materials:
Pint milk carton
or shoe box
Scissors
Glue

Directions:
1. Reproduce, color, and cut out the church. Glue it to the front of a milk carton (or shoe box).
2. If using a shoe box, cut a 2" slit in the top.
3. Reproduce and cut out the children patterns, one for each child. Each child should decorate a boy or girl face.
4. Let children drop their decorated faces in the box, indicating their desire to give themselves to God.

Church

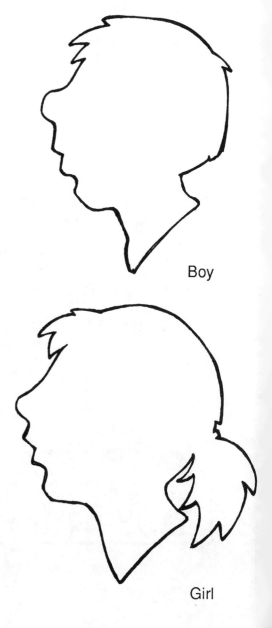

Boy

Girl

SS380

A COUPON BOOK TO GIVE

There are other things we can give to God besides money, such as our time and ourselves. Talk to the children about this, and have each of them make this coupon gift book.

Materials:
  White paper
  Stapler and staples
  Crayons

Directions:
1. Reproduce, color, and cut out the three pages below.
2. Fold the pages on the dotted lines and staple the book together.
3. Give the book to parents to show what you want to give them. They may "redeem" the coupons any time they choose.

↑FOLD

Shining Star Publications, Copyright © 1993
SS3801

GIFT BASKET

Let each child make this pretty basket, then deliver some to nursing home residents or shut-ins. This will help teach the children that it is better to give than to receive. Plan to sing some songs as the baskets are handed out.

Materials:
White paper or construction paper
Glue
Scissors
Crayons
Candy coins

Directions:
1. Reproduce the basket pattern for each child.
2. Color and cut it out.
3. Fold sides up on the dotted lines. Glue the tabs to the sides.
4. Glue the handle to the top sides of the basket.
5. Fill with candy coins or chocolates wrapped in gold and silver foil.

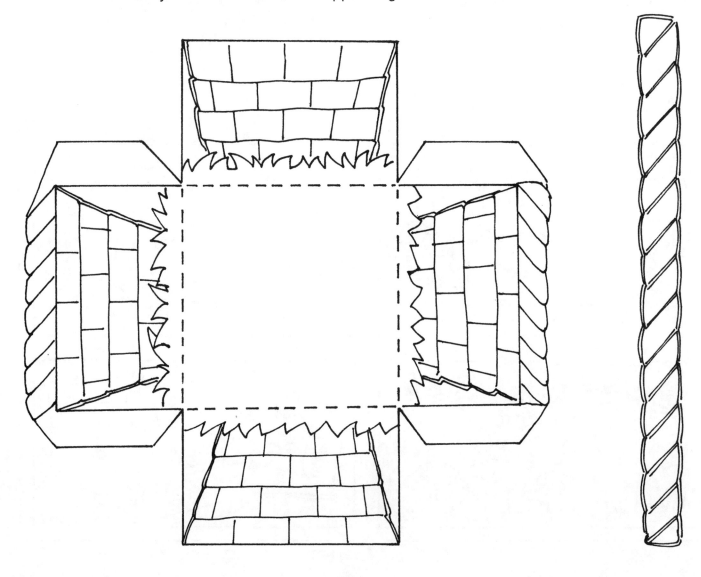

THANK YOU, GOD, FOR JESUS

Matthew 21:1-11; Luke 19:29-38; John 12:12-19

Use the pop-out pictures on pages 74-76 with this story.

People in the city of Jerusalem were feeling very excited! Jesus was on His way to Jerusalem with His helpers. Two of Jesus' helpers went to look for a donkey. Jesus had told them where to find the donkey, tied by the village gate. He had told His helpers to untie it and bring it to Him. If anyone asked what they were doing, they were to say that the Lord needed the donkey.

When the disciples brought the donkey, Jesus sat on it. Slowly He rode the donkey into the city. When the people saw Jesus coming, they began to shout with joy. They laid down palm tree branches in the road. Some people laid their coats in His path. The crowds followed Jesus. The leaders of the people were angry. They did not like the people being thankful for Jesus!

Shining Star Publications, Copyright © 1993 SS3801

POP-OUT PICTURES

Materials:
  Scissors
  Glue

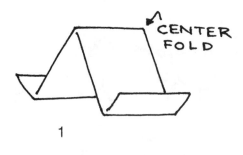

1

Directions:
1. Cut out the figures below on the heavy lines.
2. Cut out and fold the pop-out stand as shown in illustration 1 for each figure.
3. Copy the background pictures on pages 75-76 and fold them in half.
4. Glue one tab of a pop-out stand on the background picture on page 75 as shown in illustration 2.
5. Glue the top of the figure of the two disciples below to the pop-out tab. Fold the bottom of the figure on the dotted lines and glue it to the picture as shown in illustration 3.
6. Glue two pop-out stands and the figures of Jesus and the crowd to the picture on page 76 in the same way.

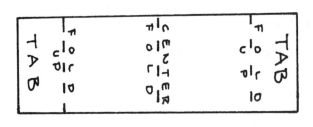

pop-out stand

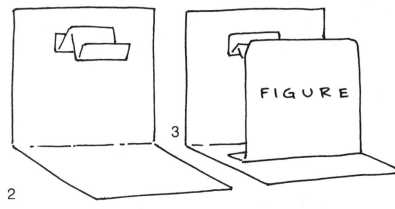

2

3

SS3801

POP-OUT PICTURES

Glue tab here.

Glue figure here.

Two of Jesus' helpers went to look for a donkey.

SS3801

POP-OUT PICTURES

Glue tab here.

Glue tab here.

Glue figure here.

Glue figure here.

Slowly Jesus rode the donkey into the city. The people laid down palm tree branches. Some people laid down their coats for the donkey to walk on.

SS3801

PIECE THE PUZZLE

Reproduce this donkey and leaf and cut into puzzle pieces for the children to put together.

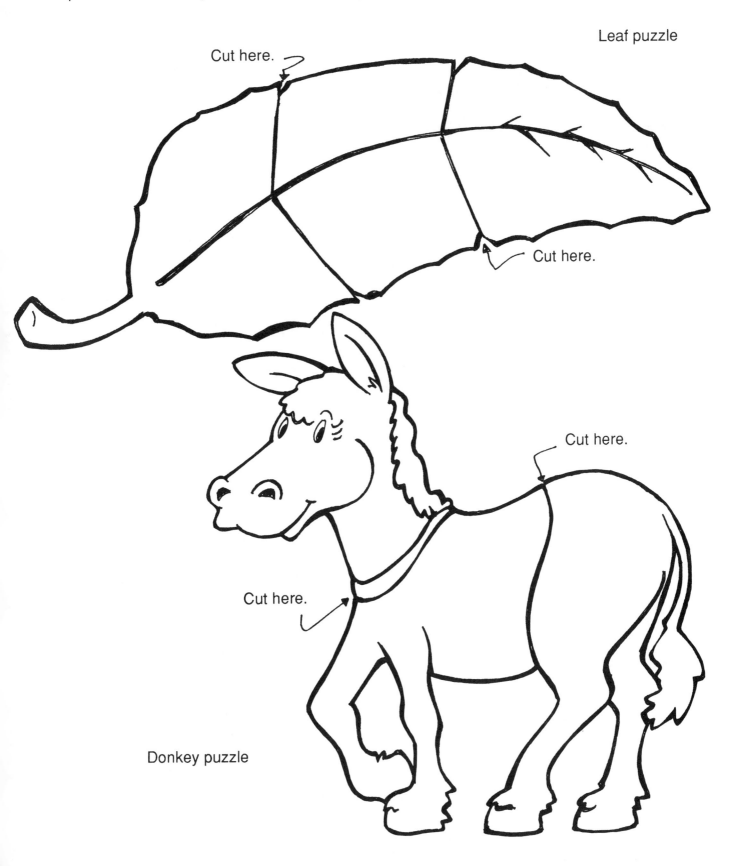

Leaf puzzle

Cut here.

Cut here.

Cut here.

Cut here.

Donkey puzzle

SS3801

A DONKEY'S TALE

Use the puppets on pages 79-80 to tell this rhyming story.

Jesus Today I asked two of my helpers to find a donkey for Me to ride.
They brought the donkey and I rode into town with My helpers by My side.

Donkey Wow, can you believe I got to carry God's Son on my back?
I held my head up high, and my hoofs went clickity-clack.

Jesus The donkey was not lazy, you see.
He wanted to do the job for Me.

Donkey Jesus, You're God's mighty Son!
Look, short people, tall people, sick people–everyone!

Jesus Boy and girls stopped their games just to see Me for awhile.
I will give each man and woman and child a smile.

Donkey They laid palm branches down on the road. They laid their coats down too.
I carried Jesus along that road as the crowd's excitement grew.

Jesus "Hosanna! Hosanna!" I heard them say.
Let them praise Me every day.

Donkey Always remember to praise God above
For sending us His Son to love!

SS3801

PAPER BAG PUPPET

Cut out this pattern and glue it to a paper bag as shown.

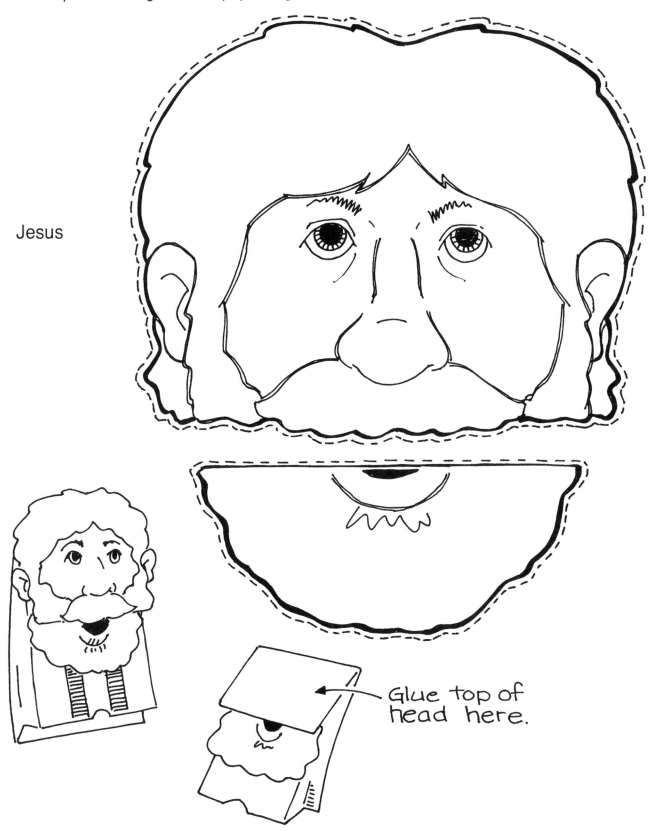

Jesus

Glue top of head here.

SS3801

PAPER BAG PUPPET

Cut out this pattern and glue it to a paper bag as shown.

Donkey

80

"TRIUMPHANT ENTRY" MAZE

Help Jesus find His way to Jerusalem.

JERUSALEM

81

SS3801

CLOTHESPIN DONKEY

Materials:
Gray construction paper
2 clip clothespins
Licorice whips
Glue or stapler and staples

Directions:
1. Reproduce and cut out this donkey pattern for each child to color.
2. Help the children clip on clothespins for the donkey legs and glue or staple a licorice tail on the donkey.

Donkey pattern

SS3801

DONKEY CRAFTS

A Donkey to Ride

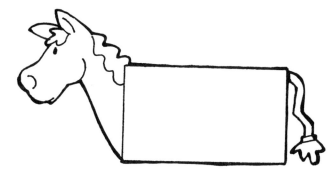

Materials:
    Box
    Poster board
    Markers
    Scissors
    Gray paper or gray paint
    Yarn
    Hot glue gun and glue or stapler and staples

Directions:
1. Use a hot glue gun or stapler to attach a large poster board donkey head to one end of a box. (You may enlarge the donkey's head on page 80.)
2. Glue or staple a rope to represent a donkey's tail at the other end.
3. Paint the box gray or cover it with gray paper. Help each child make a donkey.

Donkey Cupcake Decorations

Materials:
    Round, colored toothpicks
    Scissors
    Glue
    Markers or crayons
    Cupcakes

Directions:
1. Reproduce, color, and cut out the donkey in a circle.
2. Glue a toothpick to the back of the circle.
3. Bake some cupcakes and frost them with green icing. Stand a donkey in each cupcake.

Shining Star Publications, Copyright © 1993

SS3801

DONKEY GAMES

You may buy this game or make your own. Enlarge the donkey pattern found below on poster board. Blindfold children or put dark felt on children's sunglasses for them to wear. (They will not mind wearing the glasses as much as a blindfold.) Use yarn with a thumbtack in one end to represent the donkey's tail. Let the children try to pin the tail on the donkey.

Materials:
White paper
Scissors

Directions:
1. Reproduce this pattern for each child to color.
2. Cut out the donkey.
3. Demonstrate how children are to put their fingers through the holes to represent the donkey's legs.

Finger puppet

SS3801

HE IS RISEN

Matthew 27 and 28

Use the puppets and puppet stage on pages 86-88 with this story.

Jesus loves everyone—mothers, daddies, sisters, and brothers. But there were some people who did not love Jesus. They put Him on a cross, and He died. That was a terrible thing to do!

One of Jesus' friends, Joseph, took Jesus' body and put it in a cave. (*Hold up Joseph puppet next to paper bag cave.*) He rolled a large stone in front of the cave. (*Hold stone up and roll it in front of cave opening.*) The religious leaders put guards in front of the cave opening to make sure no one could go in or out of the cave. (*Hold guard near cave.*)

Two of Jesus' friends came to the cave early Sunday morning. (*Hold women up by cave.*) They were surprised because the stone was rolled away! (*Move stone away from cave.*) Two angels standing nearby told the women that Jesus had risen. He was alive! (*Put angels down into the bag so children can see them in the cave opening.*) The women ran to tell their friends and Jesus' helpers.

Jesus had finished the work God had sent Him to do. It was time for Him to go back to heaven. Jesus told His helpers that they were to go tell the whole world that one day everyone who obeyed Him would come to live with Him in heaven. (*Hold up Jesus, and pull Him up to heaven.*)

PAPER BAG STAGE AND PUPPETS

Materials:
- White paper
- Markers or crayons
- Craft sticks
- Glue
- Scissors
- Paper grocery bag
- Cotton

Directions:
1. Reproduce the patterns on pages 86-88. Color them and cut them out.
2. Glue the patterns of Jesus, the two angels, the guard, the women, Joseph, and the stone to craft sticks.
3. To make the stage, cut an 8" x 8" opening in the center of the grocery bag as shown.
4. Glue the cave on the inside of the bag so you can see it through the cutout space. Glue cotton to the top of the front of the bag to represent heaven.

Stage

Angel

SS3801

PUPPET PATTERNS

Women

Jesus

Stone

SS3801

PUPPET PATTERNS

Cave

Joseph

Guard

BUTTERFLY LACE CARD

The butterfly is a symbol of new life. It reminds us of how Jesus died and came alive again so our sins could be forgiven. Reproduce this butterfly for each child and use it as a sewing card to be a reminder of Jesus' love.

Materials:
Hole punch
Shoelaces or yarn
Tagboard
Markers

Directions:
1. Reproduce and cut out the butterfly pattern on tagboard for each child.
2. Color it with markers.
3. With a hole punch, put holes where indicated.
4. Use colored shoelaces or yarn to "sew" around the edge of the butterfly.

 SS3801

FINGER PUPPETS

These finger puppets may be used to retell the Resurrection and Ascension story. To use the puppets, tape the ends together and slip over fingers.

SS3801

HOME SWEET HOME

We all have homes that are special to us. Jesus has a special home for us in heaven. Draw a line from each person to the correct home on this page and page 92. Discuss the importance of our earthly homes and our heavenly home.

SS3801

HOME SWEET HOME

SS3801

A HOME PREPARED FOR YOU

Jesus is in heaven with God preparing a home for His children. Heaven is a special place where there won't be sickness, sadness, or anything bad. In heaven, we will be happy all the time. The picture below will help your children to visualize their heavenly home. Reproduce the picture for children to color. Let them glue cotton on the clouds and gold glitter on the heavenly mansion.

BUTTERFLY CRAFTS

Changing

Materials:
Construction paper
Scissors
Glue
Colored tissue paper

Directions:
1. Fold construction paper in half.
2. Draw a caterpillar as shown.
3. Cut out the caterpillar without cutting on the fold.
4. Unfold the construction paper and a butterfly shape is revealed.
5. Glue colored tissue paper on the butterfly.

If I Were a Butterfly

Materials:
Paper grocery bag
Glue
Tagboard
Colored tissue paper
Stapler and staples
Two Styrofoam™ balls
Two pipe cleaners
Construction paper

Directions:
1. To make the body of the butterfly, cut a grocery bag up the front. Cut out neck and arm openings too.
2. Cut a pair of butterfly wings from construction paper and staple them to the back of the bag.
3. Cover the bag and wings with colored tissue squares.
4. Cut two strips of construction paper and staple them together to make a headband.
5. Attach pipe cleaners to opposite sides of the headband. Attach a Styrofoam™ ball to each pipe cleaner.
6. Let children take turns wearing the costume, or make a costume for each child.

SS380

"NEW LIFE" CELEBRATION

Celebrate Jesus' resurrection with these party favors, treats, and activity.

Party Spoon Favors

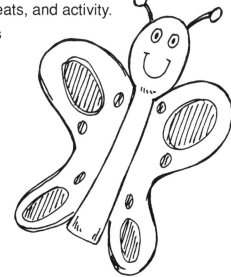

Materials:
Plastic spoons
Felt
Markers
Pipe cleaners
Glue

Directions:
1. Draw facial features on a plastic spoon with a marker.
2. Glue pipe cleaner antennae to the top of the spoon.
3. Cut butterfly wings from felt, and glue the spoon to the center. Decorate wings with colorful felt circles.

Caterpillar Fruit Salad

Materials:
Styrofoam™ egg carton
Chopped apples
Fruit yogurt
Raisins
Oranges
Pretzels

Directions:
1. Cut the lid off an egg carton.
2. Put bite-size pieces of fruit into the individual sections.
3. Spoon yogurt into the last cup. Top it with raisin "eyes" and pretzel antennae. Let children dip the fruit in the yogurt for a special treat.

SS3801

"NEW LIFE" CELEBRATION

Break the Cocoon

Materials:
Large balloon
$\frac{1}{2}$ cup flour
$\frac{1}{2}$ cup water
Off white or gray crochet thread
White paper
Scissors
Crayons or markers

Directions:
1. Mix $\frac{1}{2}$ cup flour and $\frac{1}{2}$ cup water together.
2. Spread the mixture on an inflated baloon.
3. Wrap the yarn around the balloon until it is completely covered, except for a small 2" square.
4. When dry, pop the balloon. Cut a small square in the 2" opening.
5. Fill the cocoon with candy and treats. Reproduce the butterfly below on white paper for each child and cut out. Have children color them, then put them in the cocoon.
6. Hang the cocoon from the ceiling.
7. Blindfold a child and let him try to break open the cocoon with a stick.
8. When the cocoon breaks, let the children pick up the butterflies and treats.

"He Is Risen" Invitation

You're invited to a "New Life" celebration.

Shining Star Publications, Copyright © 1993 SS3801